ALLEN PHOTOGR

CW00719723

COMPETITION STYLE

CONTENTS

INTRODUCTION

When it comes to the niceties of dress, what to wear and when, the horse sports stand supreme. Perhaps it harks back to dandyism from today's tieless Britain, but no other sport has such refined rules regarding dress.

This photo guide, on the basis that a picture is better than a thousand words, shows what riders wear for competition today. They have their own style and you will develop yours. This book is a guide to help you look the part – and win!

DRESSAGE

(*right*) Swallowtail coat, cream silk stock with breeches and gloves to match, the uniform of the dressage rider. Dressage riders, like dancers, are giving a precise performance; they should have a smiling grace and look as though they are enjoying it.

(*below*) The Advanced test dressage outfit. Simple and elegant.

(*below right*) Style at the highest level. Note the details: the cut and fit of the coat, the boots high to reach the small of the knee, the neat hair treatment; the whole as precise as an accurate half-pass.

(*right*) Another view of effortless style. The coat is midnight blue. The hat is worn perfectly, with the brim just over the eyebrow.

(*below*) An alternative dress for Advanced tests. A bowler hat could also be worn with this outfit but, beware, they do not suit everyone. So if you want to make a style statement in a bowler, be sure it is right for you. The long whip confirms that a dressage whip can be any length.

(*below right*) For tests at a lower level – Preliminary to Advanced Medium – a tweed coat, buff breeches and light brown gloves provide a less formal look. The stock follows the hunting dress known as 'ratcatcher' and distinguishes this style from the show ring, where a tie would be worn.

(*right*) Top hats vary. This one is of an average height for a dressage top hat.

(*far right*) A taller hat which suits the tall wearer. Note the well-cut coat, perfectly plain with black buttons, which has the look of Savile Row about it. It would also be suitable for a three-day-event rider at Badminton or Burghley.

(*below right*) The shallower-crowned hat came from the continent and the English, with their strict dress code for hunting, looked down on it at first. Today it is accepted, but it is a demanding style. The hairstyle must be immaculate so that the hat forms part of the total ensemble. Here, with intuitive personal style, the rider has made a feature of her hat by tipping it well forward. The arrangement of the hair adds to the sense of pin-perfect chic.

(*below*) This young rider has chosen a shallow-crowned, straight-brimmed hat which suits her perfectly. Her image is one of well-tailored neatness. She knows she is on show as well as her horse. Full marks.

(*right*) Note the extravagant curl on the brim of this top hat. Be sure to try different styles (there are plenty to choose from) and take a friend, who will give you an honest opinion, to help you find the look that is right for you.

(*far right*) A well-tied cream stock, with a plain horizontal pin completes a picture of classic elegance and style. To be in style, learn how to tie a stock correctly, neatly and securely (see diagram below).

How to Tie a Stock

1. The untied stock. First, pass the collar-part round the neck from front to back and fasten the front button-hole to the top button of the shirt.

2. Push the right-hand end through the slot in the stock and bring both ends of the stock on to the chest.

3. Tie a right-over-left knot, pulling the knot close to the neck. One end will lie over the right shoulder and the other will lie flat on the chest.

4. The end on the chest is now folded upwards and over the left shoulder.

5. Bring the other end down and pass it across and through the loop, or fold, of the end over the left shoulder.

6. Pull the ends tightly with an upward pull.

7. Fold the ends down over the tight knot and straighten the stock. Fasten with a stock pin inserted horizontally through both ends of the stock and the shirt.

8. This alternative effect is achieved by pulling the second knot less tightly than that in Diagram 6 and arranging both sides so that the head of the second knot forms the base of the triangle.

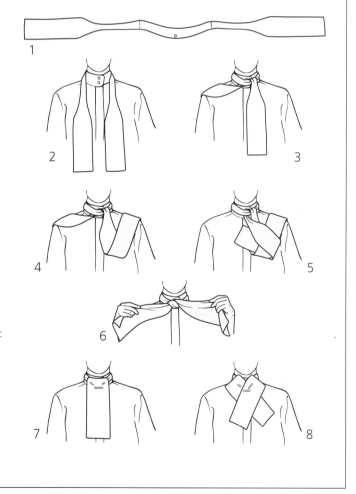

(*right*) Popular with showjumpers, the white collar and tie is invading the dressage arena. It is not a style enhancer. It undermines the tradition of the tailcoat which dates from about 1820, when the day wear of the English country gentleman was adopted by the fashionable Regency man. The stock, properly tied, is more elegant and right with the tailcoat; don't throw it out yet, even if the collar and tie is easier and quicker.

(*below*) The appearance of manufacturers' names and logos is widespread in this age of sponsorship. The motor-racing world pioneered this. The collar of this coat is discreetly outlined in red, white and blue piping, the rider's international colours, and discretion is the key. If an international pocket badge is worn, a flashy collar should not compete with it, a mistake made by the British Dressage Team in the 2002 World Equestrian Games. Alas, their lack of sartorial style was matched by their performance!

(*below right*) A white stock, off-white breeches and, again, a slightly taller hat for a tall rider. The use of a waistcoat 'piece' – which buttons

on to the inside of the coat – rather than a waistcoat proper, means that riders can consider a slightly heavier cloth for the tail coat which will cut, hang and, consequently, look much better than a thinner material. And, since the tail coat is only put on minutes before the test and does not have to be worn for any length of time, this is worth considering.

(*right*) Give a thought to the colour of your breeches. Consider a softer cream, champagne or very pale beige. Pure white is highly reflective but it can work, as it does here: white shirt (subtly patterned and short-sleeved for cool elegance), white stock, white gloves, white saddlecloth. The only colour is in the prized Union Jack – very clever.

(*right centre*) Here, off-white breeches are teamed with a cream silk stock tied in a straight style. The half-rolled sleeves add an air of casual elegance while working the horse in.

(*below left*) A four-buttoned navy-blue jacket worn with a top hat. The usual topper height of 4¼ in looks well with a short jacket and can be worn at all levels up to Advanced; the jacket must be black or navy blue.

(*below right*) Freedom of choice is rare in dressage but, for ladies, it does extend to how the hair is arranged. Develop your own style but make sure it works under a top hat or cap. If it is long, then you must secure it attractively. Sometimes a false bun is the answer, but avoid overlarge fixings and bows. There is nothing false here and the effect is neat and elegant.

(*right*) An immaculate coat worn by a rider at junior international level. The two-button style reveals the waist-coat points in the manner of the swallowtail coat. The hunting cap (now known as a beagle) has a high crown, which is attractive.

(*far right*) The same dress at adult level. The cutaway style of the two-button coat has a swept back elegance but you must have the figure for it, like this rider who is tall and slim (the camera puts on 7 lb). This style creates a deeper V at the neck, which makes it essential to secure the ends of the stock with small safety pins or they will fly free and upset concentration, perhaps at a vital moment.

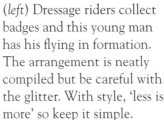

(*left*) Dressage riders collect badges and this young man has his flying in formation. The arrangement is neatly compiled but be careful with the glitter. With style, 'less is more' so keep it simple.

(*right*) Do not miss the chance to display your sense of individual style when working in. The austere black and white of the arena makes way for elegant casual clothes, colours and fabrics carefully put together. But this rider prefers to stick to black. The look of a ballet dancer on horseback gives her a high fashion lead.

(*right*) You can keep it as simple as you like. Here a dazzling white polo shirt twinned with stone-grey breeches is coolly elegant. The clothes are spotlessly clean, an essential ingredient for equestrian fashion.

(*right*) She is on a horse, but she wears the look of Bond Street or the Burlington Arcade. She has put her clothes together very carefully and it shows.

(*far right*) Dressage is a visual thing – sometimes audio-visual when it is dressage to music. Dressage riders should refine their sense of style in and out of the arena and dare to be different. Consider this cloak, with echoes of the Household Cavalry, for a cold morning.

(*right*) 'Dare to be different? A brown hat? Well, I'm not sure…' You could not wear it under today's rules as black is assumed with a black or navy-blue coat. But would a brown swallowtail coat not look good? Yes, surely. One day perhaps.

(*above*) Casual hats, other than baseball caps, are rarely worn these days. Dressage riders miss a style opportunity if they go bareheaded, especially in hot weather. It is Aachen, and it is hot, but this brown straw is 'cool'!

(*below*) Bootscape. A bewildering array of boots for the dressage rider. Choose carefully. Manufacturers have wide ranges of shapes and foot sizes. Do not economize here, spend money, pay for quality boots and make them last by ensuring they are properly cleaned and polished.

(*below*) Dressage boots reach just below the knee, and have the tops shaped to show off the leg as dressage riders ride long. Here is elegant proof of the old saying 'a good leg for a boot'. Field boots have lace-up fronts and this splendid pair is in black patent leather.

EVENTING

THE DRESSAGE PHASE

The dress for all classes (including Novice three-day events) matches hunting dress.

(*right*) A hunting man in Leicestershire; this is the Shires and he wears the uniform of a true Meltonian: black swallowtail coat with checked waistcoat, white breeches, top boots with spurs, white stock and tall, black top hat. Dressed like this he could enter the dressage arena at Badminton and be in perfect style.

(*below right*) The dress for a lady competing in Advanced and international events. Her breeches are buff and she wears plain black butcher boots. Only gentlemen wear mahogany top boots and white breeches with the swallowtail coat.

(*below*) In the arena at Burghley. The tall hat is a traditional hunting style. If you can find a real silk hunting topper do not hesitate to wear it. The finish is superb and it outshines the synthetic version every time. The eventing topper is taller than the low hats worn for pure dressage but the same rule applies: make sure it suits you.

(*right*) Ladies wear black or dark-blue coats, buff breeches and plain black boots. Gentlemen can opt for scarlet (or black) with white breeches and mahogany top boots, hunting cap or top hat. This is the ladies' version.

THE CROSS-COUNTRY PHASE

(*below left and right*) For cross country the influence switches from the hunting field to the racecourse and competitors dress like jockeys, from race-style hat covers and shirts down to white breeches and top boots for the boys.

(*below*) The key is to find colours that work for you then emphasize them by repeating them. The colour co-ordination of this rider's and horse's clothing has been carefully chosen.

(*above*) A perfectly matched outfit and an immaculate rider. The single colour for the shirt and hat cover works well, and it is teamed with fawn breeches, well-fitting boots and a neat hair treatment.

(*below*) A blue and white quartered cap and a white shirt embraced by a body protector in corresponding blue. Strong distinctive colours. The stock is recommended for safety purposes but also adds a touch of tradition and style.

(*below*) The rules require approved body protectors. The choice of olive green and pink looks well against 'cross country' backgrounds. The body protector extends to cover the lower back. A neck protector is also worn.

(*below*) The influence of sponsors extends to the cross-country outfit. Work with your sponsors to capitalize on the company's colours and logo. Here the corporate red, white and black are cleverly portrayed.

International colours, this time of Sweden, uniform yet distinctive.

(*above*) If you wear a contrasting outfit, put the colour in the hat. Your connections will see it as you speed round the course. This is an excellent colour and a very well turned out rider. Note the cream stock.

(*above right*) Research your choice of hat carefully, and always go for safety first. This is a new design, pioneered by Mr and Mrs Chris Collins, after their daughter had a fall from a horse, resulting in a serious head injury. The hat, like a motor cyclist's helmet, covers much more of the head than standard crash hats. At the British Equestrian Trade Association Fair, it won the Safety and Security Award. It has its own streamlined style. It is endorsed by the six-times Badminton winner Lucinda Green.

(*below*) Lucinda's style influenced another aspect – the Veterinary Inspection. She abandoned horsey clothes in favour of smart casual and wore her Australian hats.

Others followed the World Champion's example and now the Veterinary Inspection is something of a fashion parade.

THE SHOWJUMPING PHASE

(*below*) Eventing's growth, and British success, owes much to hunting and especially the late Duke of Beaufort KG, GCVO, MFH, who established the Badminton three-day event on his land in 1949. It is a happy reminder to see hunting dress in the showjumping phase. Note the white breeches (rather than buff) and mahogany top boots.

(*below*) The equivalent dress for ladies: a neat black (or dark blue) coat, plain black boots and white stock. Again, the showjumper's white breeches are worn rather than the buff of the hunting field. The impression is one of efficiency in dress.

SHOWJUMPING

(*right*) Showjumpers today. 'Competitors must at all times wear correct riding clothes, complete with jackets … whenever they enter the arena', the BSJA Rules insist. Jackets vary: the emerald green is the sponsor's choice, and you cannot miss it! White breeches and mahogany top boots, collar and tie, sometimes cream rather than white, are standard. The appearance of the sponsor's name on the collar may be good for business but it is not stylish.

(*right below*) A lady rider from the United States in team colours on Nation's Cup day in Dublin. A perfectly tailored scarlet coat, white breeches, 'American' stand-up collar, plain black boots and hunt cap. She looks the part in every way. The English tradition is for lady internationals to wear black or navy-blue coats in international competitions (again, the influence of the hunting field), while the men wear red. Overseas countries keep things uniform, with all team members in the same national colour.

(*far right*) Another stylish lady showjumper. A lightweight scarlet coat, with four buttons, dazzling white breeches, high-cut black boots, neat hunt cap and, instead of a stock, a white shirt with a high collar of precise fit. Style indeed.

(*right*) A well-cut coat from the back. Observe the two vents, the length, which is just right in relation to the saddle, and the neat short spurs.

(*right*)The sponsorship of the sport has seen some rare colours emerge. The Marketing Manager who plumped for purple claimed instant recognition for his company: a smart move.

(*below left*) 'Competitors are not permitted to carry or wear any form of advertising material while in the arena, except for logos in accordance with Rule 102.8 and sashes presented in the arena at the time, or as leading horse or rider indicators.' So states the BSJA Rule Book. There is no doubt who supplies this rider's horsepower, but the gentleman is not a British rider and perhaps the rules of other countries are different.

(*below centre*) Your sponsor is important to you…show it. Wear the corporate livery and keep in touch with your sponsor, ask what you can do to further the cause!

(*below right*) A subtle shift in colour from dark blue or black to dark grey, and it is most welcome. This is a classic outfit, no frills or fuss, letters or logos, a winning case for the 'keep it simple' rule.

(*right*) Another classic – the perfect outfit for a lady show-jumper. The blue shirt with high white neckband is a simple substitute for the stock, neatly elegant and secure, much better than the white collar and tie, which rarely remains neatly tied.

(*far right*) A good plain coat. All the more so as the rider has allowed the Union Jack pocket badge to draw the eye by standing alone. She has not confounded and confused it with horsey baubles and other frippery. The crash hat has its harness secured at more than two points – a popular design, properly worn.

(*below left*) A wider collar band can work and this is a good example. But thinking of hair treatment – how will she get that hair under her hat…?

(*below centre*) This coat collar just catches the eye. It is not too deep so there is just a touch of colour, which is all you need. Big collars with a slab of gaudy colour look awful.

(*below right*) Equestrian underwear, soft yet durable, prevents chafing and adds to your riding comfort. Look around for something that suits you.

(*right*) A junior showjumper wearing a plain black coat with black velvet collar, white showjumping shirt and white breeches. The gloves have reinforced fingers to improve rein grip.

(*far right*) Another junior showjumper in a smart dark-green coat with a black velvet collar. In the saddle she looks the part and means business. The jodhpurs clip neatly and securely over the black jodhpur boots.

(*below left*) This junior wears a plain navy-blue coat, off-white jodhpurs and gloves, a white showjumping shirt and black velvet crash hat; a traditional outfit that is hard to beat.

(*below right*) A body protector worn over the matching jacket for this small showjumper shows the growing emphasis on riding safety, but choose the right colour and it can form part of your 'look'.

ENDURANCE RIDING

(*below*)The British Endurance Riding Association asks that riders should be smartly turned out. But individual dress style, linked to comfort and efficiency in a ride, which may be from 40 to 100 miles, is plain to see. For those cold morning starts, this rider designed her own outfit – a zipped fleeced jacket and cotton Lycra riding tights in a panda pattern for instant recognition. She uses the flexible caged stirrups so that she can wear heelless footwear if she chooses to, has a monitor wire running to electrodes under the saddle to keep tabs on her horse's heart rate, and wears the essential ventilated helmet of approved safety standard.

(*right above*) This rider carries a map slung over her shoulder and a Shoof boot to go over the horse's foot in case he loses a shoe. Her bum bag contains a bandage, a mini first-aid kit, a space blanket and a compass. A decision to wear bold single-colour outfits, as opposed to a patchwork of unrelated shades, is shrewd; this rider will catch the eye from a good distance.

HOMEWARD BOUND

Make sure your horse looks stylish with colour co-ordinated rugs and bandages when you take him home after the competition.

Ride in style … good luck!

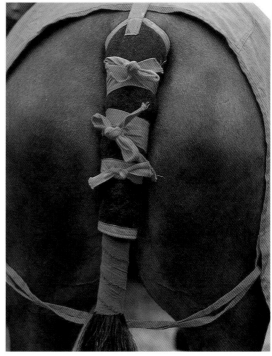

DRESS RULES

The following rules are summaries of the official rules of each discipline's governing body: British Dressage; British Eventing; the British Show Jumping Association. See the relevant rule books for full details.

DRESSAGE

Coats Advanced tests: uniform or tail coat with top hat, or black/navy-blue coat, correctly tied white/cream stock with hunting cap, bowler or crash cap. Preliminary to Advanced Medium tests: uniform or black/navy blue or tweed coat with correctly tied stock, white American collar or shirt and tie, hunting cap, bowler or crash cap.

Breeches/jodhpurs Must be white, cream or beige, except when worn to comply with official uniform.

Gloves Must be worn.

Boots Must be black or brown and may be top boots or jodhpur boots. Gaiters may be worn providing they are of identical leather to the boots and have no decoration.

Spurs Must be worn from Medium level upwards and must be made of metal. The band round the heel must be smooth and there must be a shank on the back of the heel pointing toward the rear. There is no restriction on the type of shank and rowels permitted provided that they are fitted vertically and are free to rotate. Rowels which have points must have rounded ends.

Whips It is permitted to carry a whip in all national classes except area festivals, semi-finals, regional championships, championships or at the request of the selectors. A whip may always be carried by ladies riding side-saddle. A whip may be of any length.

EVENTING

Advanced, international three-day events and CICs (international one-day events). Advanced one-day events and international championship one-day events only.

Dressage

Ladies	*Gentlemen*
Top hat	Top hat
Black or dark-blue tailcoat	Black or red tailcoat
White hunting stock	White hunting stock
Gloves	Gloves
Buff (fawn) breeches	White breeches
Plain black boots	Black boots with mahogany tops

Note Spurs are only compulsory in Advanced and all FEI dressage tests. They must be of smooth metal, the shank no more than 3.5 cm long, blunt without rowels. Whips are not allowed to be carried during a dressage test.

Cross Country

Ladies	*Gentlemen*
Hard hat (see Rule 52) with cover	Hard hat (see Rule 52) with cover
Sweater or shirt	Sweater or shirt
Hunting stock (recommended for safety purposes)	Hunting stock (recommended for safety purposes)

Ladies	Gentlemen
Buff breeches	White breeches with top boots or
Black boots	buff breeches with plain black boots.
Body protector (BETA standard approved)	Body protector (BETA standard approved)

Note Whips must not exceed 75 cm in length.

Showjumping

Ladies	Gentlemen
Hard hat (see Rule 52)	Hard hat (see Rule 52)
with black or dark-blue cover	with black or dark-blue cover
Black or dark-blue coat	Black or red coat
White hunting stock	White hunting stock
Gloves	Gloves
Buff (fawn) breeches	White breeches with top boots (black with mahogany tops)
Plain black boots	or buff breeches with plain black boots.

Note Uniform can be worn. For dressage classes at lower levels, the top hat and tailcoat gives way to hunting cap and a black or dark-blue coat. A tweed coat with a coloured stock or collar and tie may be worn at Novice and Junior one-day events.

SHOWJUMPING

Competitors must wear correct riding clothes complete with jackets whenever they enter the arena.

Long hair Long hair should be worn in a net or secured in such a way as not to hang below the collar.

Hats All riders must wear protective headgear to quality assurance standards which includes a retaining harness secured to the shell at more than two points. See Rule 267. Hats or helmets requiring covers must be worn with a plain dark-coloured peaked cover.

Jackets Traditionally tailored jackets must be worn in the arena.

Shirts Only white or pastel-coloured shirts with white collars and ties or hunting stocks. Ladies may wear white or pastel-coloured showjumping shirts with high white collars, but without a stock or tie. However, coloured ties or stocks may be worn with tweed hacking jackets. Juniors who are members of the Pony Club may wear Pony Club ties regardless of the colour of their jackets.

Breeches/jodhpurs These must be white, pale yellow or fawn.

Boots Riding or jodhpur boots. Plain black leather gaiters (not suede), but in the traditional riding-boot style with black jodhpur boots may be worn, but not when red coats are compulsory. This is an unwritten rule in international competitions and those in the UK when the prize money exceeds £100.

Gloves Optional.

Body protectors Optional. Juniors may wear body protectors either under or over their jackets but adults must wear them underneath the jacket.

Not permitted Polo neck sweaters, chaps and half chaps.

ENDURANCE RIDING

There are no rigorous dress rules – although the rider is expected to be smartly turned out – but a hard hat of acceptable British Standards must be worn, and whips may not exceed 30 in.

If a rider chooses footwear without a heel, caged stirrups must be used.

British Library Cataloguing-in-Publication Data.
A catalogue record for this book is available from the British Library

ISBN 0.85131.783.9

Published in Great Britain in 2003 by
J. A. Allen an imprint of Robert Hale Ltd.,
Clerkenwell House, 45–47 Clerkenwell Green,
London EC1R 0HT

Design and Typesetting by Paul Saunders
Series editor Jane Lake
Colour processing by Tenon & Polert Colour Processing Ltd., Hong Kong
Printed in China by Midas Printing International Ltd